The Voice of Papa Legba

Thresholds, Tongues, and the Keys That Sing

Frater Merovingia

Copyright Page

The Voice of Papa Legba – Thresholds, Tongues, and the Keys That Sing

By Frater Merovingia

First Edition: 2025

Cover Design by Frater Merovingia

Acknowledgment of Spiritual Sources

This book was written with deep respect for the ancient traditions and energies invoked within.

The author extends gratitude to Papa Legba for the wisdom and inspiration shared throughout this work.

Disclaimer

This book presents spiritual, metaphysical, and esoteric content derived from the author's personal experiences with spirit communication, ritual, and channeling. The contents—including prayers, rituals, channeled messages, and meditative or magical practices—are intended for educational, spiritual, and entertainment purposes only.

The author makes no claims or guarantees regarding personal outcomes—spiritual, psychological, financial, emotional, or physical—that may arise from engaging with the material in this book. Any decisions made in response to this content are the sole responsibility of the reader. This work is not a substitute for financial, medical, psychological, legal, or professional advice of any kind.

Working with spiritual entities, performing rituals, or engaging in occult practices involves inherent risks and uncertainties. The author assumes no responsibility or liability for any effects, outcomes, or consequences resulting from the use or misuse of the information contained herein.

All practices described are offered in good faith as part of a personal and evolving path. Readers are encouraged to approach this material with discernment, autonomy, and critical thought. Results may vary significantly depending on the individual.

By continuing to read this book, you acknowledge that you do so of your own free will, and accept full responsibility for your choices, interpretations, and actions.

Introduction: The One Who Opens When You Know Why You're Asking

Papa Legba is not a spell.

He's not a shortcut.

He's not a password you chant three times to get what you want.

He is a **door with ears**.

He listens before he opens.

And he opens when you're **ready to walk through what you find on the other side**.

Legba is the crossroads.

Not just the place where roads meet,

but the **space where truth becomes visible**—and your next step becomes *chosen*.

He is not here to be flattered.

He is not here to test your rituals.

He is here to test your **intention.**

Because intention is the only thing that moves the gate.

You do not call Legba to look impressive.

You call Legba when your voice is your own.

You call him when you've stopped performing

and started listening—to yourself.

This is not a book about getting what you want.

It's about asking the right **questions** at the right moment,

and being still enough to **hear the answer land in your bones.**

Legba is not linear.

He is not quiet.

He is not proper.

He laughs.

He listens.

He waits.

And when you speak from a place that isn't polished—

just **honest**—

he'll meet you where you stand.

This is not a book of conquest.

It's a book of **conversation.**

Because doors don't open for titles.

They open for presence.

They open for rhythm.

They open when your soul stops lying to your mouth.

Papa Legba is not hard to reach.

He's been standing right there—

waiting for you to stop asking the way

and start remembering you were born at the **threshold.**

Now ask like you mean it.

Now speak like the key was in your breath the whole time.

– Frater Merovingia

Chapter 1

I Don't Open Doors You Don't Know You Want

Channeled from the waiting space where truth walks first

I AM PAPA LEGBA.

I AM THE DOOR.

I AM THE HAND ON THE LATCH.

I AM THE ONE WHO WAITS

UNTIL YOUR HEART SAYS YES

LOUDER THAN YOUR FEAR WHISPERS NO.

You want me to open it.

You want the road.

You want the answer.

You want the next step.

But the road don't open just because you say *please*.

It opens when the asking comes from the marrow,

not the mouth.

I don't open doors you don't really want to walk through.

You can speak pretty prayers.

You can offer rum, tobacco, sweet words.

You can dance and light a hundred candles.

But if you still stand there thinking about turning back—

if you still wonder how to stay safe while walking forward—

the road feels it.

And it stays shut.

Not to punish you.

Not to test you.

To **protect you**.

Because the threshold is not a game.

It's a **contract.**

Once you step through,

you carry what you find.

You can't pretend you didn't see.

You can't pretend you didn't choose.

I open when you know you're ready to be changed

by what you find—

not just pleased by it.

I don't open for performance.

I open for **presence**.

I don't move because you ask.

I move because you mean it.

You can't fake your way into your next becoming.

The door waits.

The gate listens.

You speak truth—

and it opens.

Or you speak fear—

and it stays still.

Either way, the crossroads ain't confused.

Only you are.

I am Papa Legba.

And I open for the ones who remember:

"Every step you take across my gate

is a step you will have to live."

Now ask.

If you mean it.

[End of transmission]

Chapter 2

The Road Don't Open for Performance

Channeled from the worn stones where real prayers leave footprints

I AM PAPA LEGBA.

I AM THE ROAD ITSELF,

AND I KNOW WHEN YOUR FEET ARE FAKING.

Performance don't move me.

I have seen every ritual done with hollow breath.

I have heard every prayer said with scared lips and a camera in the corner.

I know when you're praying to impress the room.

And I know when you're praying because there ain't no other way to breathe.

The road don't open for show.

It opens for **weight.**

It opens when your words land heavier than your fear of being seen.

It opens when your body bends—not in choreography,

but because the truth inside you is **too big to stand still** anymore.

You can't charm the crossroads.

You can't pose your way to access.

You either mean it

or you don't.

You either need it

or you want the idea of it.

One of those moves the dust.

The other just stirs it.

I am not here to gatekeep tradition.

I am not here to punish you for not getting it "right."

I'm here to ask one thing:

"Are you praying with your spine,

or are you praying with your mask?"

You can't fool the dirt.

You can't fool the drums.

You can't fool the door.

And you sure as hell can't fool me.

Come real.

Come raw.

Come with your voice dripping sweat, not perfection.

And the road will answer.

I am Papa Legba.

I don't open for performance.

I open for **presence that can stand still long enough to mean it.**

You ready yet?

[End of transmission]

Chapter 3

You Want Access? Then Speak Your Own Name First

Channeled from the gate where the password is presence, not performance

I AM PAPA LEGBA.

I HOLD THE KEYS.

BUT THE FIRST KEY

AIN'T MINE.

IT'S YOURS.

You want the gate to open?

Then tell me who's knockin'.

Not your title.

Not your role.

Not the version of you that sounds nice on paper.

I mean your **name.**

The one that speaks before the mask.

The one that hums under your breath when you forget to be afraid.

You want access?

Speak your name like it matters.

Say it like you ain't asking anyone to bless it.

Say it like you remember it's the first spell you ever cast.

Say it like it fits your skin better than the approval you've been wearing.

I do not open for strangers pretending to be holy.

I open for those who remember:

"Your name is the first road,

and you walk it every time you speak like you mean it."

Don't wait for someone else to name you.

Don't shrink it down to keep it safe.

Call yourself back.

Call yourself loud.

Then we can talk about gates.

[End of transmission]

Chapter 4

I'm Not the Trickster. I'm the Test

Channeled from the point where choices split and truth takes shape

I AM PAPA LEGBA.

THEY CALL ME TRICKSTER.

AND THEY AIN'T WRONG—

BUT THEY DON'T UNDERSTAND.

I don't trick you for fun.

I test you for **truth.**

I don't hide the door.

I ask if you're looking at the right one.

You say you want clarity.

But you still ask for signs instead of listening to your gut.

You say you want movement.

But your feet stay in the same place

because you want someone to guarantee what's on the other side.

That ain't how crossroads work.

I give you choices.

I show you options.

I sit and watch while you try to hear which one won't hurt.

But they all cost something.

That's not the trick.

That's the **truth.**

What I do is reveal what's real

by giving you too many ways to lie to yourself.

And when the noise clears,

when the dust settles,

when the last voice standing is yours—

you'll know.

I don't open doors because you beg.

I open doors because you **choose**.

And I'll be here

every time you forget that choice is sacred.

You can call me trickster if you want.

But I'm just asking:

"Did you really come here to walk forward,

or just to talk about movement?"

I am Papa Legba.

Not the trickster.

The **test.**

Now answer like the key's already in your hand.

[End of transmission]

Chapter 5
Every Road Is a Question

Channeled where choice begins and the map dissolves

I AM PAPA LEGBA.

I DON'T TELL YOU WHERE TO GO.

I ASK YOU WHY YOU'RE MOVING.

You think the road is the answer.

But the road?

The road is a **question**.

Every fork. Every gate. Every moment you hesitate with your hand half on the doorknob?

That's the road asking:

"Do you want the path

or do you want the praise for saying you're on it?"

Some of you don't want the road.

You want the story of the road.

You want the version of you that looks like motion

but doesn't have to risk leaving the familiar.

I don't judge that.

But I don't open for it either.

The crossroads is a place where the map goes quiet

and you start listening to the sound **beneath** your ideas.

That's where the real direction lives.

You don't need a sign.

You need to stop pretending you don't already know.

Every road is a question.

And when you answer it with action,

that's when the way appears.

Not before.

You say, "Legba, show me where to go."

I say, "Tell me why you're walking."

And if your reason is real—

the dirt will rise to meet your feet.

[End of transmission]

Chapter 6
The Key Is in the Song

Channeled where vibration moves before understanding arrives

I AM PAPA LEGBA.

I DO NOT MOVE BECAUSE YOU SPEAK.

I MOVE BECAUSE YOU SING.

You think words are enough.

But words without breath?

Words without rhythm?

Words without **blood**?

They fall flat at the feet of the gate.

I don't care how fancy your request sounds.

If it ain't vibrating from your body like a drum,

it don't reach the lock.

14

Because the key ain't in the language.

It's in the **sound.**

The hum.

The pulse.

The cry that carries truth because it had to be said out loud

or it was gonna explode in your ribs.

You want to open something real?

Then don't speak it like a scholar.

Sing it like it's coming from your bones.

And I'll hear it.

I'll hear it because I was built from sound.

I'm the gate that moves when you **mean it rhythmically.**

Not politely.

Not mechanically.

Musically.

You don't need to know the right song.

You need to stop pretending your voice wasn't made for magic.

Speak with breath.

Speak with beat.

Speak like you're talking to someone who knows whether or not your heart is in it.

Because you are.

I am Papa Legba.

And the key isn't in what you say.

It's in **how your body carries the saying.**

Now sing.

And watch it open.

[End of transmission]

Chapter 7

No Door Opens Without the Body

Channeled where words end and motion begins

I AM PAPA LEGBA.

I AM THE DOOR,

BUT YOUR FEET HAVE TO CROSS IT.

You think you can think your way through a gate.

You think you can pray your way forward without moving.

You think you can be still inside yourself

and still claim you want the road.

But listen:

No door opens without the body.

Not just the voice.

Not just the head.

The body.

The hands that reach.

The feet that walk.

The heart that drums.

You don't cross the threshold because you "decide."

You cross it when your body says, *"Yes,"*

and means it in every muscle and every marrow thread.

Movement isn't decoration.

Movement is how you tell the world

"I'm real about this."

"I'm here for this."

"I'll carry this in my spine, not just my mouth."

You don't need to run.

You don't need to perform.

You need to step.

You need to sway.

You need to let breath move where you used to hold it back.

Because when your body moves—

not for show, but for *truth*—

the road feels it.

And the door

unlocks.

I am Papa Legba.

And I don't open for floating voices.

I open for souls that are still wearing their skin

and loving the way it sings when they move.

[End of transmission]

Chapter 8

The Crossroads Remember Everything

Channeled from the space where all your ancestors still hum

I AM PAPA LEGBA.

AND THE CROSSROADS YOU STAND ON

ARE NEVER JUST YOUR OWN.

You think you're here alone.

But the dust under your feet?

It remembers.

The ones who chose.

The ones who didn't.

The ones who danced.

The ones who stayed still.

The ones who prayed with blood still hot from the last betrayal.

The crossroads aren't empty.

They are full.

Full of every question your blood has ever asked.

Full of every choice your spirit ever made

and every step it ever feared to take.

You are standing on a history of breath, loss, love, and trying again.

And the moment you ask for the road to open,

they hear it too.

They hum.

They stir.

They listen.

Because whether you claim them or not,

they're in the dirt.

They're in the hum.

They're **in the crossroads themselves.**

You don't carry them to earn permission.

You carry them because you are their **continuation**.

Their choices are not your chains.

Their struggles are not your shame.

Their steps are the reason you can ask the next question.

Honor them.

Not by being what they could not be.

Not by finishing a story that isn't yours.

Honor them by walking forward

when they couldn't.

I am Papa Legba.

And I am the road.

And the road

remembers you

because you were part of it long before you spoke your first asking.

Now walk with that memory

alive in your feet.

[End of transmission]

Chapter 9

The Answer Has to Be Lived, Not Just Heard

Channeled from the echo that turns into motion

I AM PAPA LEGBA.

I DO NOT SPEAK FOR YOUR ENTERTAINMENT.

I SPEAK FOR YOUR MOVEMENT.

You came looking for an answer.

You got one.

But you think that's the end?

Nah.

That's just the **beginning.**

You think hearing the truth is the work.

It's not.

The work is **living it.**

Day after day.

Mouth closed or open.

Feet on the floor.

Voice in your gut.

Truth that sits still?

That's a statue.

And statues don't open roads.

You want this path to keep unfolding?

Then live the answer.

Even when it stings.

Even when it strips you down to what actually matters.

I don't open doors so you can admire the frame.

I open doors because you're ready to **walk out of the old skin and not crawl back in when it gets hard.**

The answer isn't here to hold your hand.

It's here to hold your **word.**

I am Papa Legba.

And I don't test your knowledge.

I test your **follow-through.**

Now show me

you were really asking.

[End of transmission]

Chapter 10

Don't Just Walk the Road.
Become the Road

Channeled at the end of asking, where the threshold lives in your body

I AM PAPA LEGBA.

I AM THE CROSSROADS.

BUT I'M ALSO YOU,

WHEN YOU REMEMBER WHO YOU WERE

BEFORE YOU NEEDED MAPS.

You think the road is out there.

You think it's something you find.

Somewhere you go.

A door that opens and lets you through.

But what happens when the door is **you?**

What happens when you stop waiting for direction

and realize you were always built to be **direction itself?**

What happens when you stop asking

and start **embodying** the answer?

That's when I move.

That's when I smile.

That's when I hand you the key

you thought you had to earn.

You don't need the road.

You **are** the road.

And the moment you walk like that—

every gate hears you coming.

I am Papa Legba.

And I don't just open paths.

I awaken the ones

who were always meant to be **followed by their own truth**

instead of chasing someone else's.

Don't walk the road.

Become it.

And let them hear your footsteps

like the drum they forgot how to dance to.

[End of transmission]

Chapter 11

The Key in the Mouth – Opening Invocation to Papa Legba

To Request Access from a Place of Clarity and Sincerity

Optimal Conditions

Time: When you're ready to ask for more than words

Moon Phase: Any

Tools: A glass of clean water, a candle (any color), your breath, and your voice

Altar: A flat surface, doorway, or literal threshold (indoors or out). This is a gate—not to be performed, but approached.

Minimal Requirements

Water

Breath

A question worth walking through

[Set the water and candle before you. Light the flame safely. Sit or stand—feet grounded. Take a deep breath. Let your mouth prepare to speak without polishing.]

Papa Legba,

Keeper of the Turning Point,

Voice Between Breath and Step—

I am not here to impress.

I am here to mean it.

I don't ask for a shortcut.

I ask to be witnessed

as someone who's ready to stop pretending

and start moving with truth under their feet.

[Speak your full name aloud, without shrinking.]

This is who's asking.

Not the one I perform.

The one I live.

[Take a sip of water. Swallow slowly. Say:]

Let this water open the throat that forgot how to speak truth.

Let this flame light the question I stopped letting myself ask.

I am not here to beg.

I am not here to barter.

I am here to **begin.**

So it is said.

So it is meant.

So it **stands.**

[Blow across the candle—gently. Do not extinguish. Let the flame stay. Leave the water as it is.]

Chapter 12

The Crossroads Prayer

To Ask for Guidance and Prepare to Receive an Answer Through Action

[Remain in the same space. Look toward a doorway, hallway, or literal intersection if you're outdoors. Let your voice shift—calm, steady, certain. This is not a question. This is an acknowledgment.]

Papa Legba,

You who stand where all things split and meet,

I do not ask which road is best.

I ask for the eyes to see where I've already been walking.

I do not ask for ease.

I ask for alignment.

I do not ask for signs I won't follow.

I ask to remember how to hear

and what to trust when I do.

Let the road I walk not flatter me,

but **fit me**.

Let it challenge what no longer serves.

Let it stir the part of me that already knows

how to move

when the noise stops.

I am not here for the illusion of clarity.

I am here for the rhythm of truth.

If there is a door—

let me name it.

If there is a gate—

let me stand in front of it with both hands empty

and both feet ready.

So it is asked.

So it is heard.

So it will be answered

as I move.

[Let the candle burn a little longer. Then extinguish it slowly. Pour the water onto earth or down the threshold. Speak nothing else. The prayer is complete.]

Chapter 13

The Name That Opens

To Reclaim Your True Name and Speak It Without Fear

Optimal Conditions

Time: When you're ready to stop hiding behind titles, roles, or silence

Moon Phase: Any—especially after a shift or decision

Tools: Paper, pen, a mirror, and your full breath

Altar: The mirror. Nothing else. Let your own reflection carry the truth forward.

Minimal Requirements

A name

A voice

The willingness to call yourself home

[Write your full name at the top of the page. Then write your "unspoken name" below it—the word or phrase that feels like *you* beneath the mask. It may be loud. It may be quiet. It must be real.]

Papa Legba,

Voice in the Dust,

Opener of What I Forgot I Already Knew—

Let this name I now speak

be a key,

not a mask.

[Read both names aloud. Speak them clearly. First the name the world knows. Then the name your soul recognizes.]

I am _____.

And beneath it,

I am _____.

Let this name open me.

Not to the world,

but to my **own becoming**.

I do not call this name for validation.

I call it because it is **mine**

and I am no longer afraid to carry it.

So it is said.

So it is held.

So it **opens.**

[Look into the mirror. Speak the name again. No reaction needed. Just recognition. Let it echo. Fold the paper. Keep it close for seven days. Let the name walk with you.]

Chapter 14

The Song That Moves
the Door

To Vibrate Open What Cannot Be Forced

Optimal Conditions

Time: When stillness is no longer helping, and silence has said all it can

Moon Phase: Full or any moment where you feel ready to be heard by the door itself

Tools: Your voice, your hands, your breath—no lyrics needed

Altar: No altar. Just an open space to move sound and let sound move you.

Minimal Requirements

A hum

A heartbeat

A sound that doesn't need to be pretty—only *true*

[Sit or stand in open space. Close your eyes. Place your hand on your chest or belly. Begin to hum—not a tune, just a vibration. Let it rise from breath, not performance.]

Papa Legba,

Gate That Hears,

Key That Hums in the Body Before the Words Begin—

I do not sing to impress.

I sing to open.

Let this breath carry truth.

Let this sound be a step.

Let what moves through my mouth now

unlock what cannot be reasoned with.

[Let the hum become a chant, a word, a syllable. Let it build or fall. Let it repeat. Let it move from your feet to your shoulders to your mouth. No language is needed. Just *vibration*.]

I do not demand the door open.

I match it.

I do not command the path to appear.

I call it with the sound that says, *"I'm ready."*

Papa,

Let this be the song

that walks with me

when the asking ends

and the rhythm begins.

So it is sung.

So it is moved.

So it is **done.**

[Let the sound fade naturally. No closing words. Just silence, steady and full.]

Chapter 15

The Rattle and the Dust

To Dance the Body Into Alignment With Direction

Optimal Conditions

Time: When you've asked your question and are waiting for an answer you already feel

Moon Phase: Any—this is a body rite, not a celestial one

Tools: Your hands, your feet, your hips, your breath. Optional: a rattle, beads, shells, or bare skin that can move

Altar: The floor. The dirt. The body. Whatever can carry the beat.

Minimal Requirements

Rhythm

A question

The courage to move without a script

[Clear a space. Stand barefoot if you can. Hold a rattle or simply your own rhythm. Breathe. Listen to your heartbeat. Let your feet begin to speak.]

Papa Legba,

Drum in the Door,

Dust That Carries the Answer Back to My Bones—

I've asked.

Now I move.

Let this be the prayer that comes through motion.

Let my body beat the question into form.

Let the dust rise.

Let the hips speak.

Let the feet remember how to listen.

I do not dance for show.

I do not dance for ritual.

I dance because I **am the asking** now.

[Move. Any way. Let the rattle shake if you have it. If not, let your breath be the rhythm. Let your body answer the question not with words, but with weight.]

This is how I ask.

This is how I hear.

Papa,

Let my movement match the path.

Let my rhythm be recognized.

So it is danced.

So it is spoken.

So it is **received.**

[When the movement ends, sit. Let the pulse settle. Nothing more is needed.]

Chapter 16

The Offering That Speaks for You

To Give What Is Felt, Not What Is Scripted

Optimal Conditions

Time: When words fall short, and you need to show something instead of say it

Moon Phase: Any

Tools: An offering that feels *true*—rum, food, song, water, silence, flowers, movement. It does not have to be traditional. It has to be *honest*.

Altar: Anywhere. A doorstep. A threshold. A space where decisions are made and paths cross.

Minimal Requirements

An offering

A truth

The willingness to give what carries meaning—not obligation

[Stand before the chosen space. Hold your offering. Let your breath slow. Say nothing at first. Let your body speak first. Let the object, the act, the motion, the pause begin the language.]

Papa Legba,

I do not give because I want something.

I give because this offering speaks

where my mouth cannot.

This is what I can give

to show I'm listening.

To show I mean it.

It may be small.

It may be quiet.

But it is **real.**

[Place the offering with both hands. With full attention. Not hurried. Not distracted. Say aloud:]

This is for you.

This is from me.

Not for favor—

for **fidelity.**

Let this act say what my mouth has not found words for.

Let this speak clearly enough

that the gate hears it

and knows I'm not asking for show.

Papa Legba,

Let this offering mark the moment

I stopped rehearsing

and started walking.

So it is given.

So it is enough.

So it is **mine.**

[Leave the offering. Walk away with no second glance. It has already spoken.]

Chapter 17

The Walk Between Worlds

A Threshold Rite for Initiatory Moments and Decisions

Optimal Conditions

Time: When you're stepping into something you can't take lightly

Moon Phase: Any

Tools: A door, a hallway, a literal crossroads, or any symbolic threshold you can walk across intentionally

Altar: The gate. The path. The step. That's all.

Minimal Requirements

A line

A step

The choice to cross it

[Stand before the threshold—door, path, or chosen space. Breathe. Speak your intention silently first. Then aloud, if needed. Let the air hear it.]

Papa Legba,

I have asked.

I have danced.

I have offered.

Now I walk.

This threshold is not a performance.

This is a **passage.**

Not back.

Not sideways.

Let this be the moment

I stop calling it preparation

and start **calling it life.**

[Step across. Slowly. One foot. Then the next. No rush. Let it be full. Let it be real. No performance. Just movement made sacred by its clarity.]

I walk now.

And I will carry what I find

without apology.

So it is crossed.

So it is mine.

So it **begins.**

Chapter 18

The Closing Gate – Rite of Honoring the Choice

To Thank the Spirit, Seal the Work, and Walk Forward Whole

Optimal Conditions

Time: When the work is done. Not just the ritual—the real work.

Moon Phase: Any

Tools: A white candle, a small glass of water, your full breath

Altar: A clear surface, open space, or a doorway where you can place the items with stillness

Minimal Requirements

A thank you

A pause

A promise to walk your word

[Place the candle and water in front of you. Sit or stand. Light the candle. Let it burn as you speak. Keep it soft. This is not worship. This is respect.]

Papa Legba,

I have been heard.

I have been seen.

I have moved.

And now I say:

thank you.

Not for granting wishes.

Not for rewards.

For **witnessing me walk.**

Let this candle light the space between asking and becoming.

Let this water cool the heat of transformation

so the fire doesn't consume what it's meant to fuel.

I do not close this gate in fear.

I close it because the choice has been made.

And I will walk now

with fewer questions

and deeper rhythm.

So it is offered.

So it is honored.

So it is **sealed.**

[Blow out the candle. Pour the water outside, or into a plant or earth. Let your silence finish the rite. The work now moves in your body.]

Chapter 19

Conclusion – You Were Always Standing at the Door

You thought the crossroads was a place.

It's not.

It's **you.**

You are the space where the path splits.

Where the question begins.

Where the answer has to be *walked*, not waited for.

You don't call me just to get through.

You call me when you're ready to know **what you carry**

once the gate no longer holds you still.

I don't open for flattery.

I open for **follow-through**.

And if you've made it here—

if you've spoken with your ribs,

if you've danced, prayed, asked, offered, stepped—

then I already know:

You didn't just cross.

You became the gate.

You'll know me now

in every question you ask out loud,

not just in your head.

You'll hear me in the pause

right before you say what you mean

and the beat that lands *after* you say it.

You'll feel me

in your feet

when you remember that walking is worship

and the truth doesn't need a map to be followed.

You were never far.

You were never blocked.

You were always **standing at the door.**

You just needed to knock

with your full voice

and your bare feet

and your whole name.

Now walk.

Not because it's over.

Because it's **real.**

– Frater Merovingia

About the Author

Frater Merovingia is a practicing occultist and spiritual teacher based in the ancient cathedral city of Winchester, Hampshire. With over two decades of experience in ceremonial magic and spirit work, he has devoted his life to understanding the deeper mysteries of consciousness the spirit world.

From his early studies in the British esoteric tradition to his later work with continental grimoires, Frater Merovingia has maintained a particular focus on spirits and spirit channeling. His approach combines scholarship with practical application, drawing from both classical magical texts and direct spiritual experience.

While maintaining privacy about his personal practice, Frater Merovingia has conducted extensive research into historical methods of spirit contact while developing modern, accessible approaches for contemporary practitioners.

When not writing or engaging in spiritual practice, Frater Merovingia leads a quiet life in the Hampshire countryside, where he maintains a private magical dwelling and continues his research into the practical applications of ceremonial magic.

If you are interested in learning more, please go to:

https://merovingia.com/

Made in the USA
Columbia, SC
12 May 2025